To: _____

From: _____

For more information and other resources contact EDEquity Books
EDEQUITY BOOKS
8351 Elm Ave Ste. 104
Rancho Cucamonga CA 91730
U.S.A.
Toll Free: 1-877-EDEQTY1 (333-7891) Fax: 1-909-466-7705
www.edequity.com/store
ISBN 978-1-61584-431-9

courage

courageous thoughts from leaders across the nation

cour·age:

Definition: courage, mettle, spirit, resolution, tenacity mean mental or moral strength to resist opposition, danger, or hardship. courage implies firmness of mind and will in the face of danger or extreme difficulty <the courage to support unpopular causes>.

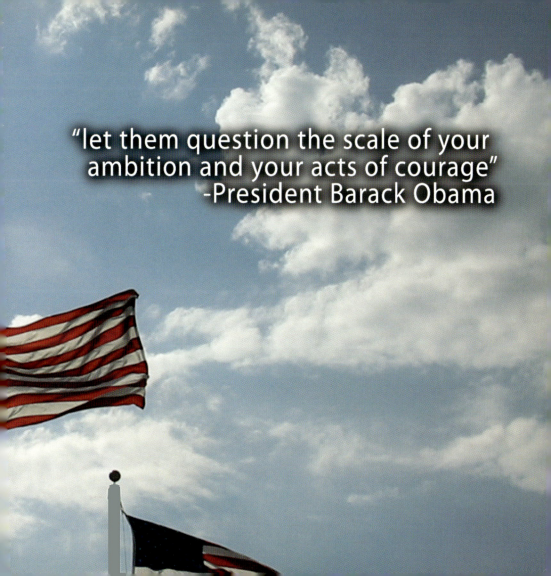

moving forward and
doing what's right for everyone
even though you know you'll
face great adversity

courage is to face fear, knowing that the challenge is real and terrifying, but to walk forward with the confidence that what you are about to do is morally and ethically the right thing to do

the willingness and the moral strength to take on an issue due to the strong belief that it is "right", even when the situation appears un-winnable

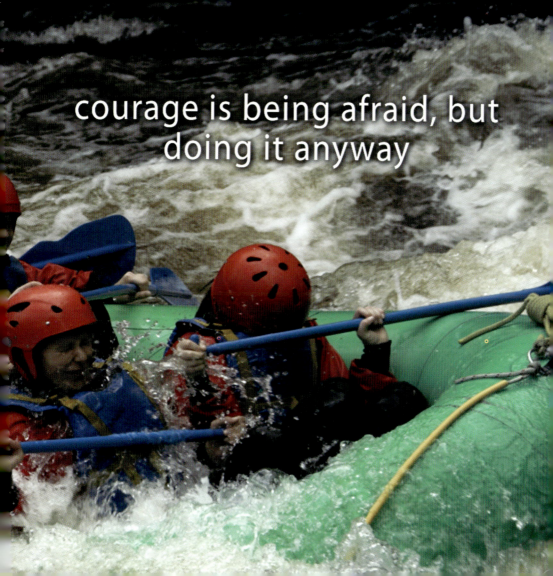

courage is being afraid, but doing it anyway

having the will and
the fortitude to face any
challenge to your principles
regardless of the consequences

courage is possessing the mental, physical or moral strength to persevere in the face of adversity

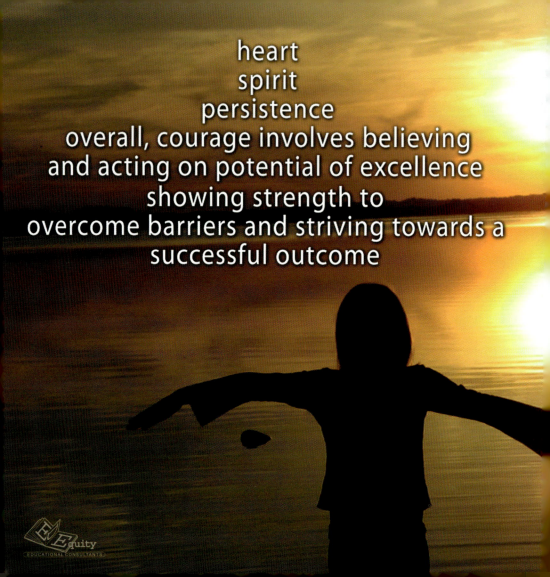

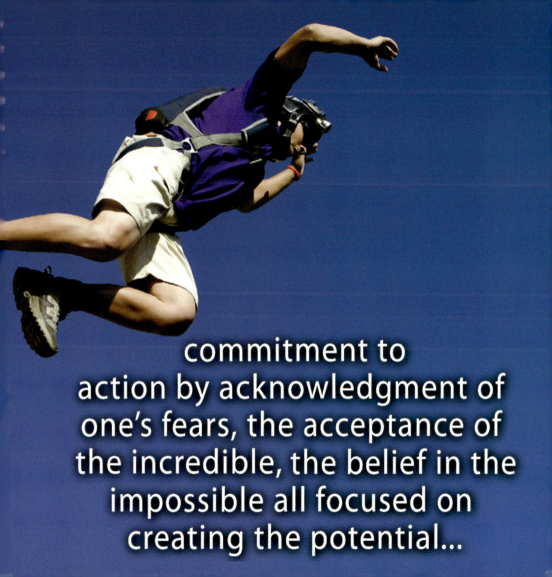

commitment to
action by acknowledgment of
one's fears, the acceptance of
the incredible, the belief in the
impossible all focused on
creating the potential...

the act of engaging in the journey of closing the persistent achievement and access gaps for all students through sharing one's vision, passion, and commitment in words and actions

having confidence to move an agenda that might be in disfavor to others of your own race

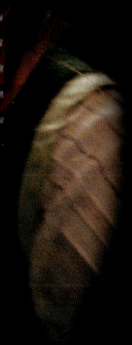

the willingness to do
something in spite of the
difficulty or challenge...
right reasons-for the kids, for
their future

ignoring the fear in
the pit of your stomach, subduing the
pounding heart and sweating palms,
losing self to speak or act to overcome
odds for a cause bigger than self in
order to shape a future that is more
humane

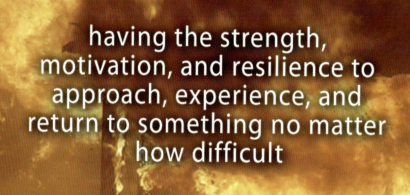

having the strength, motivation, and resilience to approach, experience, and return to something no matter how difficult

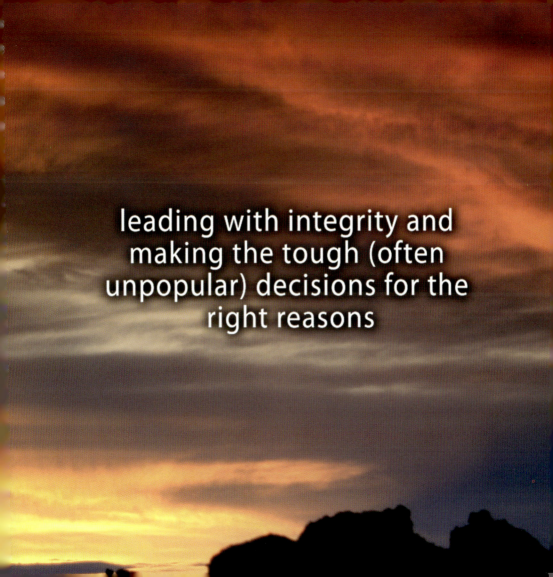

leading with integrity and making the tough (often unpopular) decisions for the right reasons

staying the course with intention and unwavering commitment to the success of all students…

"courage is an undeniable act of doing the right thing for the right reason despite personal gains and persecution from family, friends and colleagues"

-Dr. Edwin Lou Javius